TEAM SPIRIT®

SMART BOOKS FOR YOUNG FANS

THE PHILADELPHIA PHILLIES

BY
MARK STEWART

NORWOODHOUSE PRESS
CHICAGO, ILLINOIS

Norwood House Press
P.O. Box 316598
Chicago, Illinois 60631

For information regarding Norwood House Press, please visit our website at:
www.norwoodhousepress.com or call 866-565-2900.

All photos courtesy of Getty Images except the following:
SportsChrome (4, 10, 11, 12, 14, 27), Author's Collection (6, 33, 34 bottom, 36), Golden Press (7),
Black Book Partners Archives (25, 37, 41, 43 top, 45), Bowman Gum Co. (15, 40),
Topps, Inc. (18, 22, 23, 28, 35 top, 38, 42 bottom), Red Man (21), SSPC (30, 35 bottom right),
Diamond Match Co. (34 top), TCMA, Ltd (35 bottom left), Fleer Corp. (42 top),
Wilson Franks (43 bottom), Matt Richman (48).
Cover Photo: Jeff Zelevansky/Getty Images

The memorabilia and artifacts pictured in this book are presented for educational and informational purposes,
and come from the collection of the author.

Editor: Mike Kennedy
Designer: Ron Jaffe
Project Management: Black Book Partners, LLC.
Special thanks to Topps, Inc.

Library of Congress Cataloging-in-Publication Data

Stewart, Mark, 1960-
   The Philadelphia Phillies / by Mark Stewart.
       p. cm. -- (Team spirit)
   Includes bibliographical references and index.
   Summary: "A Team Spirit Baseball edition featuring the Philadelphia
Phillies that chronicles the history and accomplishments of the team.
Includes access to the Team Spirit website, which provides additional
information, updates and photos""--Provided by publisher.
   ISBN 978-1-59953-492-3 (library : alk. paper) -- ISBN 978-1-60357-372-6
(ebook) 1. Philadelphia Phillies (Baseball team)--History--Juvenile
literature. I. Title.
   GV875.P45S74 2012
   796.357'640974811--dc23
                                                         2011047975

Manufactured in the United States of America in North Mankato, Minnesota.
196N—012012

COVER PHOTO: The Phillies celebrate their 2008 championship.

TABLE OF CONTENTS

ABOUT OUR GLOSSARY

In this book, there may be several words that you are reading for the first time. Some are sports words, some are new vocabulary words, and some are familiar words that are used in an unusual way. All of these words are defined on page 46. Throughout the book, sports words appear in **bold type**. Regular vocabulary words appear in ***bold italic type***.

MEET THE PHILLIES

In the city of Philadelphia, Pennsylvania, sports fans have a lot of choices. There are *professional* teams in baseball, football, basketball, and hockey. College sports also compete for attention. The Phillies are the city's oldest team. They have been bringing together friends, families, and baseball fans since the 1800s.

The athletes who play for the Phillies come from all over the country and all over the world. Like others in the city, they help give Philadelphia its wonderful *diversity*. They also work as hard at their jobs as the people who pay to watch them play.

This book tells the story of the Phillies. Year in and year out, they do whatever they can to reach the **World Series**. And each season, people come from miles around to be part of that journey. They cheer for the Phillies when they play well—and definitely let them hear about it when they don't! That is the Philadelphia way.

Philadelphia fans cheer Ryan Howard after he scores a run.

The Phillies played their first season in 1883. By then, the game of baseball had already been popular in Philadelphia for two *generations*. A team called the Athletics first brought professional baseball to the city in the 1860s. The Athletics went out of business in 1876. For several years, baseball fans in Philadelphia did not have a **major-league** team to root for. They were happy when the Phillies joined the **National League (NL)**.

During the 1890s, the Phillies had some awesome teams and truly great players. Billy Hamilton, Ed Delahanty, and Sam Thompson formed an excellent outfield. Hamilton was baseball's greatest **leadoff hitter**. Delahanty was the game's most exciting slugger. Thompson had a strong bat and an even stronger throwing arm.

Other stars of those early clubs were catcher Jack Clements, infielder Napoleon Lajoie, and pitcher Charlie Ferguson.

In the early 1900s, John Titus, Roy Thomas, and Sherry Magee gave the Phillies another excellent outfield. It was not until 1915, however, that the team won its first **pennant**. That club was led by a young pitching ace named Grover Cleveland Alexander. Alexander, Erskine Mayer, and Eppa Rixey kept games close for Philadelphia's hitting stars, including Gavvy Cravath, Dave Bancroft, and Fred Luderus.

GROVER CLEVELAND ALEXANDER
pitcher

The Phillies fell on hard times during the 1920s, 1930s, and 1940s. They had some great hitters, including Cy Williams and Chuck Klein. But the team played in a small ballpark, and their pitchers could not tame opposing hitters.

Finally, in 1950, the Phillies assembled a group of good young pitchers. Robin Roberts and Curt Simmons were two of the NL's best starting pitchers. Jim Konstanty was the league's top relief pitcher. With the help of young hitters Richie Ashburn, Del Ennis, Granny Hamner, and Willie "Puddin' Head" Jones, the Phillies won their

LEFT: Billy Hamilton
ABOVE: Grover Cleveland Alexander

second pennant. This group went down in baseball history as the "Whiz Kids."

More ups and downs followed, including the heartbreaking 1964 season. That year, the Phillies were in first place by a wide margin with 12 games to play. Unfortunately, they lost 10 in a row and finished tied for second.

Philadelphia fans were cheering again by the late 1970s. The Phillies had a great team led by hitting stars Mike Schmidt, Greg Luzinski, Bob Boone, Larry Bowa, and Garry Maddox. Their best pitcher was Steve Carlton. After Pete Rose joined the Phillies, they claimed pennants in 1980 and 1983, and won their first World Series in 1980.

In 1993, the Phillies returned to the World Series with a group of tough, lovable players. Darren Daulton, John Kruk, and Lenny Dykstra were the team leaders, along with pitching stars Curt Schilling and Mitch "Wild Thing" Williams. Although the Phillies fell just short of a second championship, the team captured the spirit of Philadelphia—and set the stage for all of the exciting baseball to come.

LEFT: Mike Schmidt, Pete Rose, and Larry Bowa were the leaders of the 1980 Phillies.   **ABOVE**: Steve Carlton

The teams of the 1980s and early 1990s relied on a lot of older players who came to Philadelphia from other clubs. To build a winning *tradition*, a team needs to train young talent in the **minor leagues**. In turn, these players have an opportunity to form the heart of a successful team that competes for a championship year in and year out. The Phillies followed this plan to prepare for the 21st century.

Philadelphia scouted and signed many young players. Within a few years, Scott Rolen, Mike Lieberthal, Pat Burrell, and Brett Myers were making headlines in the major leagues. In the years that followed, three very important players joined the starting lineup—Jimmy Rollins, Chase Utley, and Ryan Howard. Each became an **All-Star**.

The Phillies surrounded Rollins, Utley, and Howard with more talent. Some players, such as pitcher Cole Hamels, came up through the minors. Others, including outfielder Shane Victorino and relief pitcher Brad Lidge, arrived in Philadelphia from other teams. All played their parts to perfection during the 2008 season. The Phillies won the NL pennant and defeated the Tampa Bay Rays in the World Series. Since then, the Phillies have continued to use this winning formula. By mixing "homegrown" talent with proven *veterans*, they have a chance to be the champions of baseball every year.

LEFT: Jimmy Rollins   **ABOVE**: Chase Utley

The Phillies spent 50 seasons in a ballpark known to most fans as the Baker Bowl. It fit neatly inside a rectangular city block. The left field fence was far away. The right field fence was 60 feet high but less than 300 feet from home plate. Fly balls that were easy outs in other stadiums were doubles, triples, and home runs in Philadelphia. The team's next stops were Connie Mack Stadium and Veterans Stadium.

In 2004, the Phillies moved into a new ballpark. Like many modern stadiums, it mixes old and new building styles. One feature fans love is Ashburn Alley, which is named after Richie Ashburn. He was an outfielder who was voted into the **Hall of Fame** in 1995. Ashburn Alley has souvenir shops and restaurants that make popular food, such as Philly cheesesteaks.

BY THE NUMBERS

- *The Phillies' stadium has 43,651 seats.*
- *The distance from home plate to the left field foul pole is 329 feet.*
- *The distance from home plate to the center field fence is 401 feet.*
- *The distance from home plate to the right field foul pole is 331 feet.*

Fans fill the stadium for a 2009 World Series game.

DRESSED FOR SUCCESS

The Phillies have had many different looks over the years. In 1915, when they finished in first place for the first time, they wore red uniforms at home and blue on the road. They continued to do so until Philadelphia's "Whiz Kids" won the pennant in 1950. After that, red became the color of choice. In recent years, the Phillies have rediscovered blue as an important part of their history.

For a short time in the early 1940s, the team changed its name to Blue Jays. While the jersey still read *Phillies*, a small Blue Jay patch was added to the sleeve. The new name never caught on, so the owners changed it back to Phillies.

Philadelphia has almost always featured a capital *P* on its cap. For many years, the team did the same on its jerseys. Starting in the 1940s, the club switched to *Phillies* spelled out in script lettering across the front of its shirts. That is the style the team uses today.

LEFT: Cliff Lee wears the team's 2011 road uniform.
ABOVE: Except for stripes missing from the sleeves and pants, Granny Hamner's uniform from the 1950s is almost identical to Lee's.

WE WON!

When the 1980 season began, Phillies fans had high hopes but low expectations. They knew that history was against them. Their team had been good in the past, but something had always prevented the Phillies from winning a championship. Would their 98th year turn out to be a lucky one?

The team's stars knew that luck was no substitute for experience. Pete Rose had won two championships with the Cincinnati Reds. Steve Carlton had won two championships with the St. Louis Cardinals. Tug McGraw had won a championship with the New York Mets. They joined Mike Schmidt—the league's top home run hitter—to lead the Phillies to first place in the **NL East**.

To reach the World Series, the Phillies had to beat the Houston Astros in the **playoffs**. The Astros held a 5–2 lead in the eighth inning of the final game of the series. The Phillies pulled together and made a great comeback. They won 8–7 on a hit by Garry Maddox.

The World Series against the Kansas City Royals was very close, too. After four games, the series was tied. The Royals were ahead in the ninth inning of Game 5 when Del Unser walked to the plate. He stroked a double to drive in the tying run for Philadelphia. Moments later, he scored the winning run.

Carlton got the ball to start Game 6. By the eighth inning, he began to tire. McGraw entered the contest to finish off the Royals. The reliever wiggled out of two bases-loaded

jams to secure a 4–1 victory and Philadelphia's first championship. Schmidt, who hit two homers and drove in seven runs, was named the series **Most Valuable Player (MVP)**.

LEFT: Pete Rose takes a swing. He helped lead the Phillies to the 1980 championship.   **ABOVE**: Tug McGraw jumps for joy after the last out of the 1980 World Series.

17

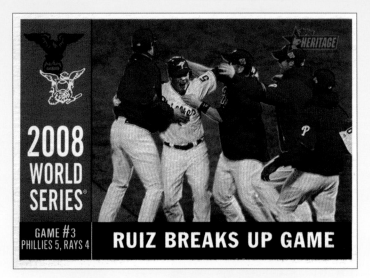

2008 WORLD SERIES

GAME #3
PHILLIES 5, RAYS 4

RUIZ BREAKS UP GAME

The club returned to the World Series again in 1983 and 1993, but both times Philadelphia fell short of another title. In 2008, the team had everything it needed to win again, including a confident leader.

When shortstop Jimmy Rollins arrived at spring training, he announced that the Phillies were the best team in the league. He and his teammates spent the next six months backing up those words.

Rollins and Shane Victorino gave the Phillies speed on the basepaths. Ryan Howard, Chase Utley, Pat Burrell, and Jayson Werth provided power at the plate. Young Cole Hamels and veteran Jamie Moyer led the pitching staff. Relief pitcher Brad Lidge slammed the door shut on 41 victories.

The Phillies defeated the Milwaukee Brewers and Los Angeles Dodgers in the playoffs to win the pennant. Next they faced the Tampa Bay Rays in the World Series. Hamels won the opening game, but the Rays took Game 2.

Catcher Carlos Ruiz was the hero in Game 3. He drove in the winning run with a 45-foot dribbler with the bases loaded. It was the first **walk-off** infield single in World Series history. The Philadelphia bats came alive in Game 4 in a 10–2 victory. Howard clubbed two home runs, and pitcher Joe Blanton got into the act with a homer of his own.

Game 5 began in a rainstorm and was halted in the 6th inning by the umpires with the score tied 2–2. The teams took the field two days later to finish. The Phillies won 4–3 on a hit by Pedro Feliz. Lidge held off the Rays in the ninth inning. It was his 48th **save** in a row, including the regular season, playoffs, and World Series.

LEFT: This trading card shows Philadelphia's celebration after Carlos Ruiz's walk-off hit.   **ABOVE**: Yeah! Brad Lidge falls to his knees after his Game 5 save gave the Phillies their first championship in nearly 30 years.

GO-TO GUYS

To be a true star in baseball, you need more than a quick bat and a strong arm. You have to be a "go-to guy"—someone the manager wants on the pitcher's mound or in the batter's box when it matters most. Fans of the Phillies have had a lot to cheer about over the years, including these great stars …

THE PIONEERS

ED DELAHANTY   Outfielder

- BORN: 10/30/1867   • DIED: 7/2/1903
- PLAYED FOR TEAM: 1888 TO 1889 & 1891 TO 1901

Pitchers hated throwing to Ed Delahanty. He would swing at any ball at any time, and he usually hit it a long way.

GROVER CLEVELAND ALEXANDER   Pitcher

- BORN: 2/26/1887   • DIED: 11/4/1950
- PLAYED FOR TEAM: 1911 TO 1917 & 1930

Grover Cleveland Alexander was called "Pete" by teammates and fans in Philadelphia. He had a sinking fastball and a sharp-breaking curveball. Alexander led the NL in wins five times with the Phillies. He set a record for **rookies** with 28 victories in 1911.

GAVVY CRAVATH — Outfielder

- **BORN:** 3/23/1881 • **DIED:** 5/23/1963 • **PLAYED FOR TEAM:** 1912 TO 1920

When Clifford "Gavvy" Cravath played, the right field fence in the Phillies' ballpark was very close to home plate. Though he was a right-handed hitter, Cravath learned how to smash balls to right field. He led the NL in home runs six times.

CHUCK KLEIN — Outfielder

- **BORN:** 10/7/1904 • **DIED:** 3/28/1958
- **PLAYED FOR TEAM:** 1928 TO 1933 & 1936 TO 1944

Chuck Klein also knew how to use Philadelphia's tiny ballpark. He was a powerful left-handed hitter who led the NL in home runs four times and won the **Triple Crown** in 1933.

ROBIN ROBERTS — Pitcher

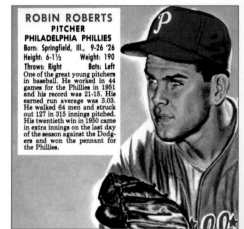

- **BORN:** 9/30/1926 • **DIED:** 5/6/2010
- **PLAYED FOR TEAM:** 1948 TO 1961

Robin Roberts threw hard and had very good control. He led the NL in wins four years in a row and in strikeouts twice. Roberts pitched more than 300 innings six times.

RICHIE ASHBURN — Outfielder

- **BORN:** 3/19/1927 • **DIED:** 9/9/1997 • **PLAYED FOR TEAM:** 1948 TO 1959

Richie Ashburn was one of the best defensive players in history. He was a good hitter, too. Ashburn led the league in batting twice.

ABOVE: Robin Roberts

21

STEVE CARLTON   Pitcher

• BORN: 12/22/1944   • PLAYED FOR TEAM: 1972 TO 1986

Steve Carlton had an excellent fastball, curveball, and slider—a pitch that bent and dipped sharply right before it reached home plate. In 1972, the Phillies finished last, but Carlton finished first in the NL in wins, strikeouts, and **earned run average (ERA)**. He won the **Cy Young Award** that year, and four times in all.

MIKE SCHMIDT   3B

PHILLIES

MIKE SCHMIDT   Third Baseman

• BORN: 9/27/1949

• PLAYED FOR TEAM: 1972 TO 1989

Mike Schmidt was the greatest slugger ever to play third base. He was also one of the best fielders. Schmidt led the league in home runs eight times and won 10 **Gold Gloves**. He was named the NL MVP three times.

JIMMY ROLLINS   Shortstop

• BORN: 11/27/1978   • FIRST YEAR WITH TEAM: 2000

Jimmy Rollins was the league's stolen base champion in his first full year with the Phillies. His speed, power, and great fielding quickly made him one of the most exciting players the team ever had. In 2007, he won the NL MVP award.

CHASE UTLEY   Second Baseman

- BORN: 12/17/1978   • FIRST YEAR WITH TEAM: 2003

In college, Chase Utley was one of the best hitters ever. After he joined the Phillies, he kept on hitting. Utley also showed he could run the bases. In 2009, he stole 23 bases without being caught once.

RYAN HOWARD   First Baseman

- BORN: 11/19/1979   • FIRST YEAR WITH TEAM: 2004

When the Phillies made Ryan Howard their everyday first baseman, they expected big things from their slugger. He delivered in a big way. Howard led the major leagues in homers twice and **runs batted in (RBIs)** three times from 2006 to 2009.

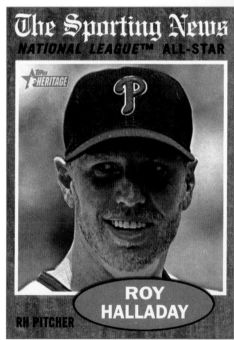

ROY HALLADAY   Pitcher

- BORN: 5/14/1977
- FIRST YEAR WITH TEAM: 2010

The Phillies traded a lot of talented young players to add Roy Halladay to their team. He rewarded them by becoming the NL's top pitcher. Halladay threw a perfect game—27 batters, 27 outs—early in the 2010 season, and then pitched a **no-hitter** in the playoffs.

LEFT: Mike Schmidt
RIGHT: Roy Halladay

Many excellent managers have called the shots from the Phillies' dugout over the years. In the 1880s, Harry Wright ran the club. Wright was a legend. Professional baseball wouldn't exist without him. Another early manager was Pat Moran. His players practiced the basics of baseball over and over until they were almost perfect. Moran's club won the pennant in 1915.

More recently, Danny Ozark, Dallas Green, Paul Owens, and Jim Fregosi helped the Phillies reach the playoffs. Ozark and Green were similar managers. Both had short tempers and were hard on their players, but their teams responded well to this type of leadership.

In 1983, Owens went from Philadelphia's business office to the dugout. He let the older players lead the younger ones, and the Phillies returned to the World Series. Ten seasons later, Fregosi led the Phillies from last place to first place, as Philadelphia won its fifth pennant.

Who was Philadelphia's most successful manager? To answer this question, fans don't have to look back very far. After taking

Charlie Manuel watches his team take batting practice.
Manuel was a power-hitting outfielder during his playing days.

the job in 2005, Charlie Manuel did nothing but win. He led the team to the top of the NL East each year from 2007 to 2011. The Phillies won two pennants and brought a World Series championship to the city in 2008.

Before Manuel arrived in Philadelphia, he was more familiar to baseball fans in Asia than in America. During his playing days, he had been a popular star in Japan. He was known for his long home runs and for always giving 100 percent. It was no surprise when the Phillies became known for the same things. Stars and substitutes loved playing for Manuel. He kept everyone relaxed and focused on winning.

ONE GREAT DAY

As the end of the 2010 baseball season neared, Roy Halladay could have looked back at the **perfect game** he had pitched for the Phillies that April and honestly said, "That was one great day!" Little did he realize that an even greater day awaited him. The Phillies faced the Cincinnati Reds in the opening round of the playoffs that October. Manager Charlie Manuel gave the ball to Halladay to start the series. It was the first time he had ever pitched in the **postseason**.

Halladay had all of his pitches working. The Cincinnati hitters went down one after another. In the fifth inning, Jay Bruce worked Halladay for a walk. He was the last Red to reach first base. In the eighth inning, with the Phillies leading 4–0, Halladay struck out two hitters and retired the third after taking a short toss from first baseman Ryan Howard.

In the ninth inning, the first two Reds popped up. The third batter was speedy Brandon Phillips. He took a big swing and hit a little

Carlos Ruiz rushes to hug Roy Halladay after his no-hitter in the 2010 playoffs.

grounder in front of home plate. Carlos Ruiz scooped the ball up and fired it to Howard for the final out. Halladay had pitched a no-hitter.

Ruiz jumped into Halladay's arms. The rest of his teammates soon joined the celebration. Halladay's no-hitter was only the second ever in postseason play. The last one was in 1956.

"I just wanted to pitch here, to pitch in the postseason," said Halladay, who was in his first year with the Phillies. "To go out and have a game like that, it's a dream come true."

When asked what he thought of his pitcher's performance, Manuel smiled and joked, "It was great managing!"

LEGEND HAS IT

PHILLIES
rick wise • pitcher

WHO HAD THE BEST 'ALL-AROUND' GAME IN PHILLIES HISTORY?

LEGEND HAS IT that Rick Wise did. In June of 1971, Wise got the job done with his arm and his bat. He pitched a no-hitter against the Cincinnati Reds and hit two home runs in the 4–0 win. No one before or since has homered twice on the same day he pitched a no-hitter. But Wise wasn't done. That September, he retired 32 batters in a row against the Chicago Cubs during an extra-inning game. Wise might have kept going had he not won the game himself with a hit in the 12th inning!

ABOVE: Rick Wise poses with a glove for his 1971 baseball card. He also got the job done with his bat!
RIGHT: Richie Ashburn takes a swing. Look out, Alice!

WHO WAS THE UNLUCKIEST PHILLIES FAN?

LEGEND HAS IT that Alice Roth was. During a 1957 game, a foul ball by Richie Ashburn hit her in the nose. The game was stopped, and Alice was placed on a stretcher. When the game restarted, Ashburn fouled off another pitch—and hit Alice again!

WHO HIT THE MOST FAMOUS HOMER IN TEAM HISTORY?

LEGEND HAS IT that Dick Sisler did. On the last day of the 1950 season, the Phillies needed to defeat the Brooklyn Dodgers to win the pennant. Philadelphia ace Robin Roberts pitched against Don Newcombe. Each gave up a run. The game went into extra innings tied 1–1. In the top of the 10th inning, Sisler came to bat with two runners on base. He hit the ball into the left field seats to give the Phillies a 4–1 victory. Sisler became world-famous. His homer was even mentioned in *The Old Man and the Sea*, a book by the famous writer Ernest Hemingway.

The Phillies and Chicago Cubs have played some wild games over the years. The wildest came on a windy day early in the 1976 season at Chicago's Wrigley Field. After three innings, the Cubs were ahead 12–1. Philadelphia manager Danny Ozark had already sent pitchers Steve Carlton, Ron Schueler, and Gene Garber to the showers.

When Mike Schmidt stepped into the batter's box with a runner on base in the fifth inning, little had changed. The score was 13–2. Chicago starter Rick Reuschel delivered a pitch, and the Philadelphia slugger hit a two-run homer. Schmidt came up again in the seventh inning and hit another home run off Reuschel. That made the score 13–7.

One inning later, Schmidt hit his third home run of the game. It came off Mike Garman and brought the Phillies to within a run, at 13–12. Philadelphia continued its comeback and moved ahead

15–13 in the ninth inning, but Chicago fought back to tie the game.

Extra innings meant that Schmidt would bat again. He faced Paul Reuschel (Rick's brother) with a runner on first. Schmidt cracked his fourth home run of the day. He joined Ed Delahanty and Chuck Klein as the only Phillies to hit that many in one game.

Amazingly, the scoring was not done. Each team added one more run that afternoon, but the Phillies held on for a crazy 18–16 victory.

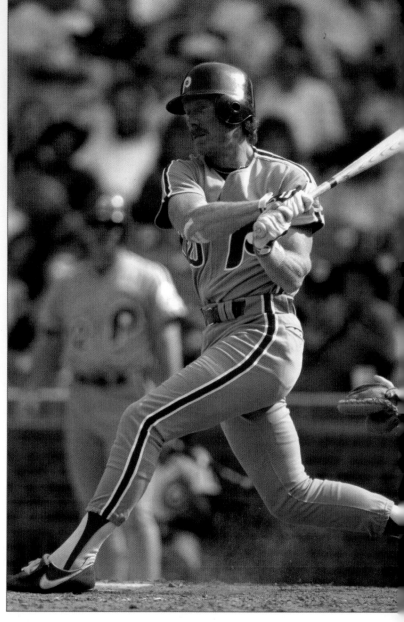

LEFT: Danny Ozark had better luck with his hitters than his pitchers against the Chicago Cubs.   **ABOVE**: Mike Schmidt bats against the Cubs in Wrigley Field.

TEAM SPIRIT

What makes a great baseball fan? The answer to this question differs from city to city. In Philadelphia, the people who buy tickets truly believe that they play a role in the team's success. If they feel one of the Phillies is not performing as well as he should, they will let him know about it! Many of the team's greatest stars have heard boos coming from the stands. They learned not to take it personally. In fact, they like fans who take the game as seriously as they do.

When it comes to supporting their team, Phillies fans are among the best in baseball. Game tickets are hard to buy at any price. Getting an extra one is like finding a needle in a haystack. Indeed, during the 2011 season, the Phillies had their 150th sellout in a row—with no end in sight!

LEFT: Fans never boo their beloved mascot, the Phillie Phanatic.
ABOVE: Fans wore this button to celebrate Philadelphia's great 1950 team.

TIMELINE

Chuck Klein

1883
The Phillies join the
National League.

1933
Chuck Klein wins
the Triple Crown.

1910
Sherry Magee wins the
NL batting championship.

1915
The Phillies win
their first pennant.

1950
The "Whiz Kids"
win the NL pennant.

In 1950, fans could celebrate
the team's pennant with a
souvenir pennant of their own.

Roy "Doc"
Halladay

DOC SHOWS PERFECT FORM

1975
Greg Luzinski leads
the NL with 120 RBIs.

2002
Bobby Abreu leads the
NL with 50 doubles.

2010
Roy Halladay pitches a
perfect game and a no-hitter.

1964
Johnny Callison wins
the All-Star Game
with a home run.

1980
The Phillies defeat the
Kansas City Royals to
win the World Series.

2008
The Phillies win their
second World Series.

Johnny
Callison

Greg
Luzinski

Eye on the Sky

During the 1930s, the Phillies did not draw many fans to the ballpark. The team did everything to get attention—including trying to catch a ball thrown from the top of a downtown office building.

Lawn Care

After William Baker bought the team in 1911, he kept a herd of sheep under the stands. They would come out and nibble the grass when it got too long. This plan lasted until 1925, when a ram butted the team's secretary. That finally convinced Baker to buy a lawnmower.

For Old Times Sake

In 2009, Cliff Lee became the second pitcher to throw a **complete game** in the World Series with 10 strikeouts and no walks. This had not happened since the very first World Series, way back in 1903.

ABOVE: The Phillies prepare to catch a ball thrown off a building in 1939.
RIGHT: Jamie Moyer throws a pitch for the Phillies in 2008.

The Big 3-0

In 2008, Jamie Moyer earned a victory over the Colorado Rockies for the first time. That made 30 teams in all that he had beaten during his career. Only five other pitchers had done this before.

Juan-Derful

From 1984 to 1987, Juan Samuel was the only player in baseball to hit 10 or more doubles, triples, and home runs in each season.

Nice Going, Dad

Jim Bunning had quite a Father's Day in 1964. He took the mound for the Phillies

and pitched a no-hitter against the New York Mets. Later in life, Bunning became a U.S. Senator for his home state of Kentucky.

Comeback Kings

In 2007, the Phillies were seven games behind the Mets with 17 games left to play. They caught fire and won the NL East. No team had ever made up so many games so late in the season.

"Playing baseball—hitting—is very difficult. But saying hello to someone is the easiest thing in the world."

▶ *SCOTT ROLEN, ON WHY HE ALWAYS TRIED TO BE POLITE TO FANS*

"From the moment I got here, I knew it was something special."

▶ *CLIFF LEE, ON THE THRILL OF PITCHING IN FRONT OF PHILLIES FANS*

"He's Mr. Everything!"

▶ *JIMMY ROLLINS, ON CHASE UTLEY, HIS LONGTIME TEAMMATE*

"I'm really proud of him. He can swing that thing, can't he?"

▶ *DICK ALLEN, ON RYAN HOWARD'S ABILITY TO HIT HOME RUNS*

"With all the *glamour* attached to hitting the ball out of the park, it takes a lot of *discipline* to go up there and just try to get a base hit."

▶ **GARRY MADDOX**, *ON BEING A SINGLES HITTER*

"His example on the field and his leadership helped to bring everybody's play up a notch."

▶ **STEVE CARLTON**, *ON THE ROLE PETE ROSE PLAYED ON THE 1980 TEAM*

LEFT: Dick Allen
RIGHT: Garry Maddox

GREAT DEBATES

People who root for the Phillies love to compare their favorite moments, teams, and players. Some debates have been going on for years! How would you settle these classic baseball arguments?

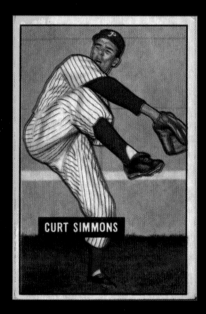

CURT SIMMONS

THE 1950 WHIZ KIDS WOULD BEAT THE 2008 PHILLIES IF THEY PLAYED IN THE WORLD SERIES ...

... because a short series is usually decided by pitching. Robin Roberts would overpower the 2008 team with his fastball. Ryan Howard and Chase Utley would have had trouble hitting Curt Simmons (LEFT), who specialized in getting out left-handed hitters. Plus the 1950 Phillies had Jim Konstanty for relief pitching. He was the MVP that year!

NO WAY! THE 2008 PHILLIES WOULD DESTROY THE 1950 CLUB ...

... because they would run wild on the bases. The 2008 team had four great base-stealers—Jimmy Rollins, Shane Victorino, Jayson Werth, and Utley. They also had hitters such as Ryan Howard and Pat Burrell, who were at their best with runners on base. That combination of speed, power, and **clutch** hitting would give the 2008 champs the edge.

... because he used his tremendous speed to help the team on offense and defense. Ashburn batted .333 and led the league in stolen bases as a rookie. He won two batting championships and topped the NL in hits three times. As a leadoff hitter, Ashburn knew that his job was to get on base. In the outfield, he caught everything hit his way. Also, in 1950 he made the most famous throw in team history—and saved the season—against the Brooklyn Dodgers.

EXCUSE ME. SHANE VICTORINO WOULD HAVE RUN CIRCLES AROUND ASHBURN ...

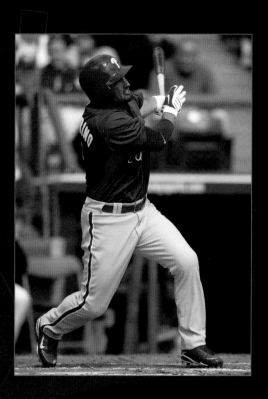

... because from the day he joined the Phillies, there was nothing he didn't do well. Like Ashburn, Victorino (RIGHT) was a great defensive player, but his arm was much stronger. Victorino used his speed to get on base, but he could also hit the ball out of the park. And he had one of the game's best nicknames: The Flyin' Hawaiian!

FOR THE RECORD

The great Phillies teams and players have left their marks on the record books. These are the "best of the best" …

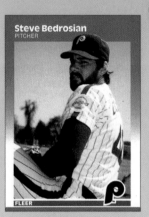

Steve Bedrosian

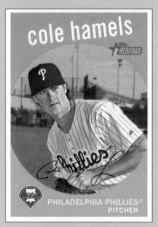

Cole Hamels

PHILLIES AWARD WINNERS

WINNER	AWARD	YEAR
Chuck Klein	Most Valuable Player	1933
Jim Konstanty	Most Valuable Player	1950
Jack Sanford	Rookie of the Year	1957
Johnny Callison	All-Star Game MVP	1964
Dick Allen	Rookie of the Year	1964
Steve Carlton	Cy Young Award	1972
Steve Carlton	Cy Young Award	1977
Steve Carlton	Cy Young Award	1980
Mike Schmidt	Most Valuable Player	1980
Mike Schmidt	World Series MVP	1980
Mike Schmidt	Most Valuable Player	1981
Steve Carlton	Cy Young Award	1982
John Denny	Cy Young Award	1983
Mike Schmidt	Most Valuable Player	1986
Steve Bedrosian	Cy Young Award	1987
Scott Rolen	Rookie of the Year	1997
Larry Bowa	Manager of the Year	2001
Ryan Howard	Rookie of the Year	2005
Ryan Howard	Most Valuable Player	2006
Jimmy Rollins	Most Valuable Player	2007
Cole Hamels	World Series MVP	2008
Roy Halladay	Cy Young Award	2010

PHILLIES ACHIEVEMENTS

ACHIEVEMENT	YEAR
NL Pennant Winners	1915
NL Pennant Winners	1950
NL East Champions	1976
NL East Champions	1977
NL East Champions	1978
NL East Champions	1980
NL Pennant Winners	1980
World Series Champions	1980
NL East First-Half Champions*	1981
NL East Champions	1983
NL Pennant Winners	1983
NL East Champions	1993
NL Pennant Winners	1993
NL East Champions	2007
NL East Champions	2008
NL Pennant Winners	2008
World Series Champions	2008
NL East Champions	2009
NL Pennant Winners	2009
NL East Champions	2010
NL East Champions	2011

The 1981 season was played with first-half and second-half division winners.

ABOVE: Scott Rolen was the National League's Rookie of the Year in 1997.
RIGHT: Del Ennis led the 1950 Phillies in home runs, batting average, and RBIs.

T he history of a baseball team is made up of many smaller stories. These stories take place all over the map—not just in the city a team calls "home." Match the pushpins on these maps to the **TEAM FACTS**, and you will begin to see the story of the Phillies unfold!

1 Philadelphia, Pennsylvania—*The Phillies have played here since 1883.*

2 Pittsburgh, Pennsylvania—*Ryan Howard won the 2006 Home Run Derby here.*

3 Boston, Massachusetts—*The Phillies played the Red Sox here in the 1915 World Series.*

4 Chicago, Illinois—*Greg Luzinski was born here.*

5 Elba, Nebraska—*Grover Cleveland Alexander was born here.*

6 Charleston, West Virginia—*John Kruk was born here.*

7 Miami, Florida—*Steve Carlton was born here.*

8 Pasadena, California—*Chase Utley was born here.*

9 Houston, Texas—*The Phillies clinched the 1980 NL pennant here.*

10 Anchorage, Alaska—*Curt Schilling was born here.*

11 Maracay, Venezuela—*Bobby Abreu was born here.*

12 San Pedro de Macoris, Dominican Republic—*Juan Samuel was born here.*

John Kruk

GLOSSARY

ALL-STAR—A player who is selected to play in baseball's annual All-Star Game.

CLUTCH—A game situation with a lot of pressure.

COMPLETE GAME—A game started and finished by the same pitcher.

CY YOUNG AWARD—The award given each year to each league's best pitcher.

DISCIPLINE—Behavior that follows rules.

DIVERSITY—Variety of cultures.

EARNED RUN AVERAGE (ERA)—A statistic that measures how many runs a pitcher gives up for every nine innings he pitches.

GENERATIONS—Periods of years roughly equal to the time it takes for a person to be born, grow up, and have children.

GLAMOUR—An attractive or exciting quality.

GOLD GLOVES—The awards given each year to baseball's best fielders.

HALL OF FAME—The museum in Cooperstown, New York, where baseball's greatest players are honored. A player voted into the Hall of Fame is sometimes called a "Hall of Famer."

LEADOFF HITTER—The first hitter in a lineup, or the first hitter in an inning.

MAJOR-LEAGUE—Belonging to the American League or National League, which make up the major leagues. Also called big-league.

MINOR LEAGUES—The many professional leagues that help develop players for the major leagues.

MOST VALUABLE PLAYER (MVP)—The award given each year to each league's top player; an MVP is also selected for the World Series and the All-Star Game.

NATIONAL LEAGUE (NL)—The older of the two major leagues; the NL began play in 1876.

NL EAST—A group of National League teams that play in the eastern part of the country.

NO-HITTER—A game in which a team does not get a hit.

PENNANT—A league championship. The term comes from the triangular flag awarded to each season's champion, beginning in the 1870s.

PERFECT GAME—A game in which no batter reaches base.

PLAYOFFS—The games played after the regular season to determine which teams will advance to the World Series. Also called the postseason.

POSTSEASON—The games played after the regular season, including the playoffs and World Series.

PROFESSIONAL—Paid to do a job; professional baseball players are paid to play.

ROOKIES—Players in their first season.

RUNS BATTED IN (RBIs)—A statistic that counts the number of runners a batter drives home.

SAVE—A statistic that relief pitchers earn when they get the final out of a close game.

TRADITION—A belief or custom that is handed down from generation to generation.

TRIPLE CROWN—An honor given to a player who leads the league in home runs, batting average, and RBIs.

VETERANS—Players who have great experience.

WALK-OFF—A hit that wins a game for the home team in the last half of the final inning.

WORLD SERIES—The world championship series played between the American League and National League pennant winners.

EXTRA INNINGS

TEAM SPIRIT introduces a great way to stay up to date with your team! Visit our **EXTRA INNINGS** link and get connected to the latest and greatest updates. **EXTRA INNINGS** serves as a young reader's ticket to an exclusive web page—with more stories, fun facts, team records, and photos of the Phillies. Content is updated during and after each season. The **EXTRA INNINGS** feature also enables readers to send comments and letters to the author! Log onto:

www.norwoodhousepress.com/library.aspx

and click on the tab: **TEAM SPIRIT** to access **EXTRA INNINGS**.

Read all the books in the series to learn more about professional sports. For a complete listing of the baseball, basketball, football, and hockey teams in the **TEAM SPIRIT** series, visit our website at:

www.norwoodhousepress.com/library.aspx

ON THE ROAD

PHILADELPHIA PHILLIES
One Citizens Bank Way
Philadelphia, Pennsylvania 19148
(215) 463-6000
philadelphia.phillies.mlb.com

NATIONAL BASEBALL
HALL OF FAME AND MUSEUM
25 Main Street
Cooperstown, New York 13326
(888) 425-5633
www.baseballhalloffame.org

ON THE BOOKSHELF

To learn more about the sport of baseball, look for these books at your library or bookstore:

• Augustyn, Adam (editor). *The Britannica Guide to Baseball*. New York, NY: Rosen Publishing, 2011.

• Dreier, David. *Baseball: How It Works*. North Mankato, MN: Capstone Press, 2010.

• Stewart, Mark. *Ultimate 10: Baseball*. New York, NY: Gareth Stevens Publishing, 2009.

INDEX

ABOUT THE AUTHOR

MARK STEWART has written more than 50 books on baseball and over 150 sports books for kids. He grew up in New York City during the 1960s rooting for the Yankees and Mets, and was lucky enough to meet players from both teams. Mark comes from a family of writers. His grandfather was Sunday Editor of *The New York Times,* and his mother was Articles Editor of *Ladies' Home Journal* and *McCall's.* Mark has profiled hundreds of athletes over the past 25 years. He has also written several books about his native New York and New Jersey, his home today. Mark is a graduate of Duke University, with a degree in history. He lives and works in a home overlooking Sandy Hook, New Jersey. You can contact Mark through the Norwood House Press website.